Draw Your
P E T !

You Can Draw

Fish!

Katie Dicker

Gareth Stevens
Publishing

Please visit our website, www.garethstevens.com. For a free color catalog of all our high-quality books, call toll free 1-800-542-2595 or fax 1-877-542-2596.

Library of Congress Cataloging-in-Publication Data

Dicker, Katie.
 You can draw fish! / Katie Dicker.
     pages cm. — (Draw your pet!)
 Includes index.
ISBN 978-1-4339-8740-3 (pbk.)
ISBN 978-1-4339-8741-0 (6-pack)
ISBN 978-1-4339-8739-7 (library binding) —
1. Fishes in art—Juvenile literature. 2. Drawing—Technique—Juvenile literature. I. Title.
 NC781.D53 2013
 743.6'7—dc23

                              2012033138

Published in 2013 by
Gareth Stevens Publishing
111 East 14th Street, Suite 349
New York, NY 10003

© 2013 Gareth Stevens Publishing

Produced for Gareth Stevens by Calcium Creative Ltd
Illustrated by Mike Lacey
Designed by Paul Myerscough
Edited by Sarah Eason and Harriet McGregor

Photo credits: Shutterstock: Bluehand 18b, Dobermaraner cover, 6b, Iliuta Goean 4, 10t, 26t, Michael C. Gray 14t, Tischenko Irina 14b, Eric Isselée 22b, 28, Kletr 24, Levent Konuk 12, Johannes Kornelius 10b, 20, 26b, DJ Mattaar 8, Mixrinho 18t, Sunsetman 22t, Vangert 16, Vlad61 6t.

Printed in the United States of America

CPSIA compliance information: Batch CW13GS: For further information contact Gareth Stevens, New York, New York at 1-800-542-2595.

Contents

You Can Draw Fish!

If you love fish, you'll love to draw them, too! Fish are beautiful creatures that make great indoor pets.

There are many different types of fish. Some fish, such as koi, can grow to be enormous and are best kept in outdoor ponds. Others, such as mollies, are smaller and perfect for keeping in indoor tanks. Some, such as clownfish, can be quite aggressive toward each other. Other fish, such as guppies, are gentle and love living in large groups. In this book, we'll teach you how to care for fish—and how to draw them, too.

Discover how to draw fish!

Follow the steps that show you how to draw each type of fish. Then draw from a photograph of your own pet to create a special pet portrait!

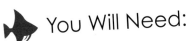 You Will Need:

- Art paper and pencils
- Eraser
- Coloring pens and/or paints and a paintbrush

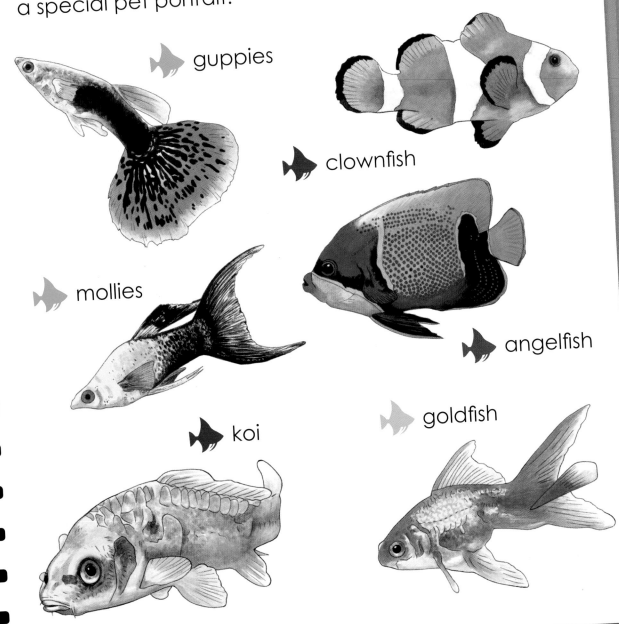

guppies

clownfish

mollies

angelfish

goldfish

koi

Angelfish

With its bright and beautiful colors, the angelfish is one of the prettiest of pet fish. Freshwater angelfish are usually kept as pets. In the wild, freshwater angelfish are found in the Amazon River in South America, where they live in large shoals.

Angelfish are famous for their gorgeous colors. The color of the fish often changes as it grows from a young fish into an adult.

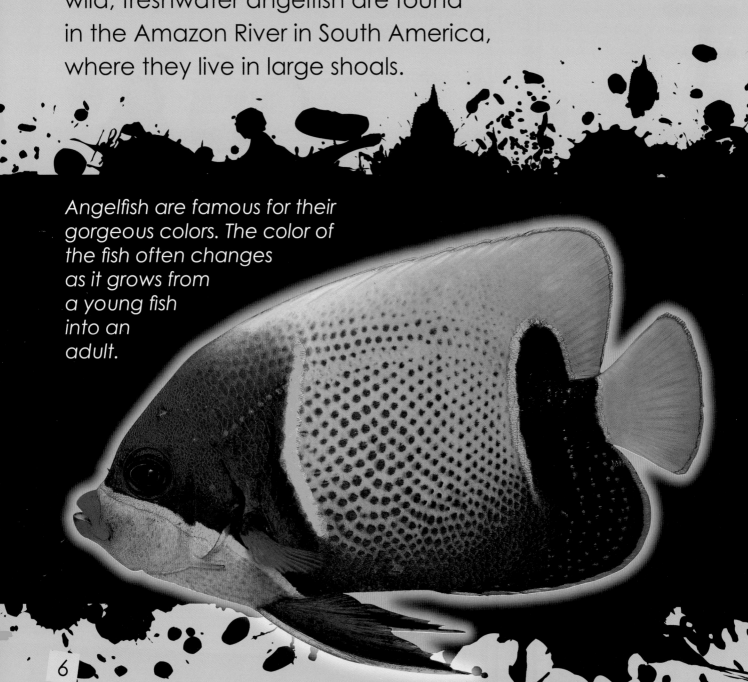

Step 1

First, draw the outline of the fish. As you draw, pay attention to the proportions of the fish's body, fins, and tail.

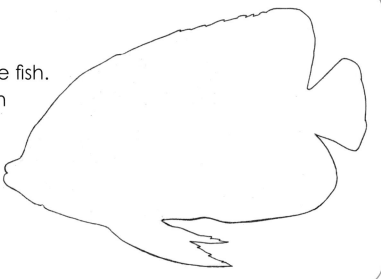

Step 2

Now add some detailed lines to your picture. Pencil the outline of the fish's mouth. Then add lines to show the two fins beneath the body.

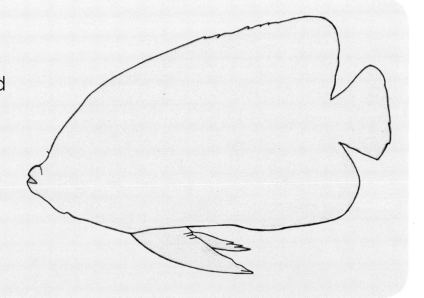

Step 3

Lightly pencil some features on the fish's face. Draw a large eye, and add lines to show the gills and the side fins. Pencil some lines to show the colored markings of the fish, too.

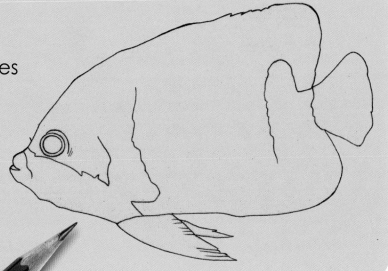

Caring for your angelfish

Angelfish live in large groups in the wild. In large fish tanks, angelfish are best kept in groups of six to eight fish. In small tanks, the fish can be kept in groups of just two to three fish.

In the wild, angelfish are active in the day and hide among plants or coral during the night. It is best to feed your angelfish when it is light to make sure they eat food regularly.

Be sure to ask your pet store for information about how to feed your angelfish. Each type of angelfish needs different types of food.

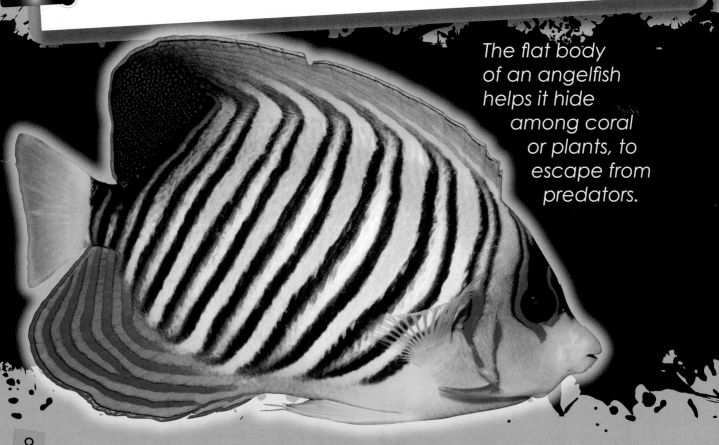

The flat body of an angelfish helps it hide among coral or plants, to escape from predators.

Step 4

Use a fine-tipped pencil to add more detail to your drawing. Show the colored spots on the side of the body. Add some feathery detail to the lower fins, too.

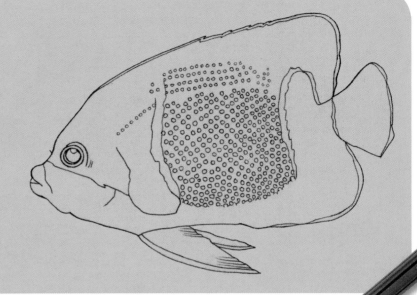

Step 5

Now you can complete your picture by adding color. Use a bright blue, yellow, and orange for the body. Add some lines of light blue and some light blue spots near the tail. Then add a white tint to the eye to make it glisten.

Clownfish

These zippy little fish have a special skill that helps them to survive. Clownfish can hide among the tentacles of deadly sea anemones without being stung! This allows them to hide from predators that would be poisoned if they swam too close to the anemone's stinging tentacles.

All clownfish are brightly-colored with three white stripes on their bodies.

Step 1

Draw the outline of your clownfish. Notice the rounded shape of the fins and tail. The mouth of the clownfish has a rounded tip, too.

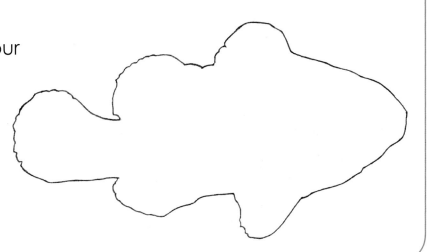

Step 2

Now add a fin to the side of the body, and use fine pencil lines to draw the tail and the fish's belly.

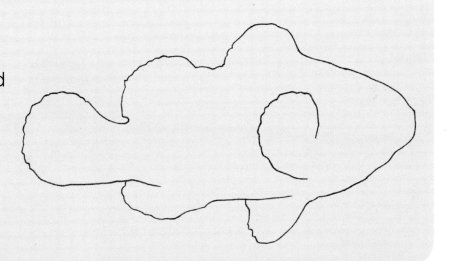

Step 3

Draw your fish's beady eye, and pencil the outline of the three white stripes.

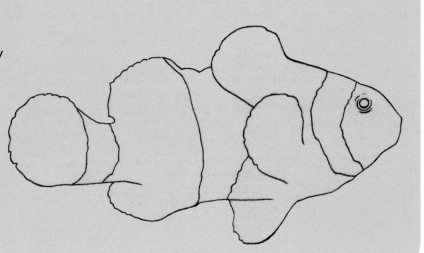

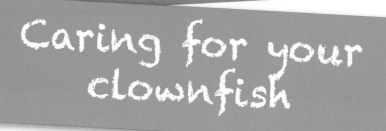

Caring for your clownfish

- Clownfish must be kept in salt water. These are ocean fish that cannot survive in a freshwater tank.

- Only keep one clownfish at a time, or just a male and female clownfish pair. Clownfish like their own space and two males or two females will fight.

- Make your fish tank as much like the ocean as you can. Clownfish love to live in an environment filled with rocks, sand, and fake plants that they can swim in and out of.

Although clownfish always fight with other clownfish, they live happily with fish of another species.

Step 4

Now add more detail to the fish's body. Add fine lines to the fins and tail, and pencil in the white and black edges.

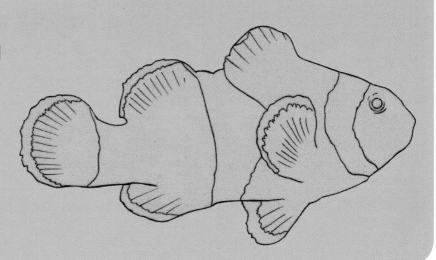

Step 5

Finally, color your fish to complete it. Choose a palette of bright orange for the body, with white and black markings. Use black for the eye, and add some lighter areas to give your drawing depth.

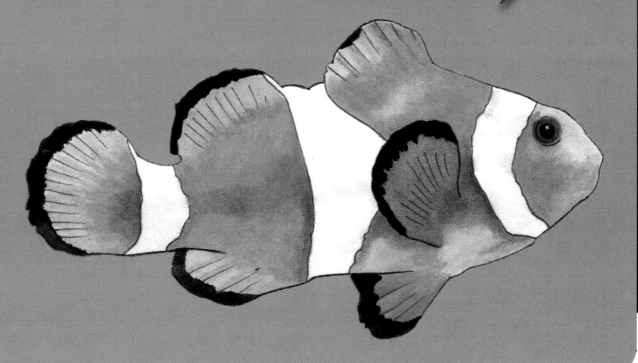

Goldfish

These are probably the most popular of all pet fish. Goldfish can be kept in an indoor fish tank, or in a pond in places that do not have cold winters. Goldfish have been kept as pets for over 1,000 years—they were kept by the ancient Chinese before they were brought to the West in the sixteenth century.

The fantail goldfish has a beautiful, long, and dainty tail.

Step 1

Draw the outline of your fish. Look carefully to be sure to include the edges of all the fins, as well as the tail.

Step 2

Now pencil some lines to show the edges of the fish's body, and add some detail to the tail and fins.

Step 3

Draw your goldfish's beady eye, and use very fine pencil lines to draw the fish's gills.

Caring for your goldfish

It is important not to heat the water of your fish tank when keeping goldfish. These are cold water fish and can go into shock or even die if their water becomes too warm.

To make sure your fish tank has enough oxygen in the water, keep at least 2 inches (5 cm) of air between the water surface and the top of the tank. Keep plants in your fish tank—they will help to keep oxygen in the water.

Feed your goldfish two or three times a day.

With its enormous eyes, the black moor goldfish is sometimes called the popeye!

Step 4

Use lots of fine pencil strokes to add detail to your drawing. Use fine lines to show the ripples on the tail and fins, then begin to draw the fish's scaly skin.

Step 5

It's time to add some color to your drawing! Use a palette of rich orange and yellow for the body, and black for the eye. Lighter shades will help to give your drawing more depth.

Guppies

Guppies are cute fish that have striking, fanned tails. The fish come from Central America. They have become popular pet fish because they are easy to care for and beautiful to watch.

Guppies are famous for their beautiful fanned tails.

Step 1

Draw the outline of your guppy as if the fish is swimming upward through the water. Notice how large the fanned tail is compared to the outline of the fish's body.

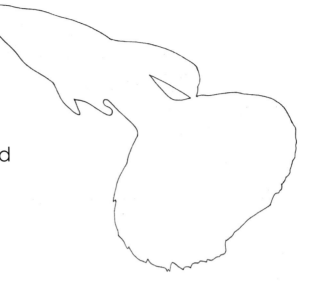

Step 2

Use steady pencil lines to draw the outline of the fish's fins. Draw the large fin on the back of the fish, and the smaller fin on its side. Add a fin about a third of the way down the side of the body.

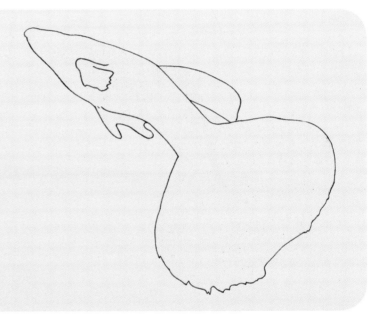

Step 3

Pencil the fish's eye, and add more detail to the body. Use fine pencil strokes to add a feathery effect to the fish's fins and tail.

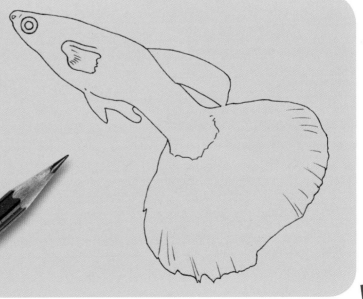

19

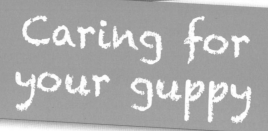

Caring for your guppy

Guppies like water temperatures at around 75–80°F (24–27°C). If kept in cooler water, the fish will not grow well.

These are gentle fish and should not be kept with more aggressive fish, such as cichlids or oscars. These larger fish will eat the guppy! Guppies do well if kept with their own species or with other nonaggressive fish.

Add some aquarium salt to your fish tank. This will help to keep your guppy healthy.

Guppies will usually live for between two and five years.

Step 4

Now add lots of detail to show the guppy's colorful markings. Be sure to draw the detail of the fanned tail. Then add fine lines to the fins, and pencil some scales on the fish's skin.

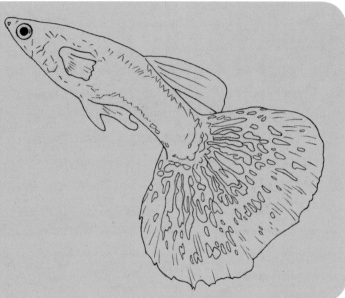

Step 5

Color your drawing to bring it to life. Use a palette of red, yellow, blue, black, green, and gray. Color the pretty pattern on the fanned tail with pink and bright yellow. Finally, add the black markings on the tail.

Koi

People in Japan love to keep a type of carp fish called koi—they have been bred there into lots of different types of koi. Today, koi are kept all over the world. They come in lots of colors, from dull gray to black, white, yellow, blue, and cream.

Big koi can grow up to 52 inches (132 cm) in length!

Step 1

First, draw the outline of your koi. The fish should seem to be swimming toward you. The tail of the fish should be curved and its fins lowered.

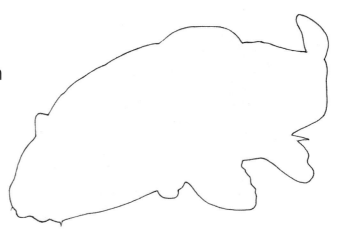

Step 2

Use pencil lines to show a fin stretching along the top of the fish's body, as well as the fins beneath the body and to its side.

Step 3

Now draw the fish's face. Draw one of the eyes, add a mouth, and two nostrils between the eyes. Use fine pencil lines to draw the gills.

23

Caring for your koi

Koi can grow to be huge! This is why they are usually kept in outdoor fishponds.

It is important to keep your pond water very clean. Many koi die because they are kept in dirty pond water. You should make sure your pond has a filter to remove any dirt from the water.

Talk to your pet store about how to feed your fish. Koi need special fish food, which you can buy from any pet stores that sell the fish.

Koi were first bred in China over 2,000 years ago. They now look a bit different than other kinds of carp, like this one.

Step 4

With a fine-tipped pencil, add some scales to the fish's skin. Draw some fine lines on the fins, too. Carefully shade the fish's huge eyes and its open mouth.

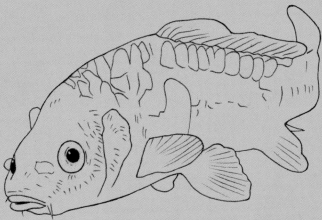

Step 5

Finish your picture by coloring it. Use a palette of yellow, gray, and white. Add detail to the scales. Light tints will also help to give your fish's skin a shimmering glow.

Mollies

Mollies are unusual fish because they can live in both freshwater and salt water. There are many different types of molly in the wild. Some live in freshwater streams. Others swim in the ocean near the seashore.

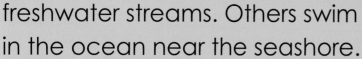

Like guppies, mollies have a long, fanned tail.

Step 1

Draw the outline of your fish's body. The fish should seem to be darting through the water. Carefully draw the fins and tail. They should appear to be sweeping backward as the fish swims forward.

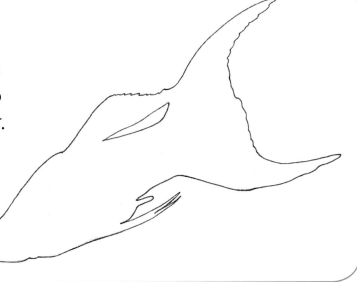

Step 2

Next, draw the edges of the fish's body. Then add the detail of the second fin on the other side of the body.

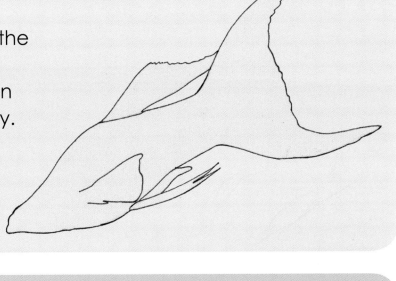

Step 3

Draw the fish's eye. Then use fine pencil strokes to give the fins and tail a feathery look.

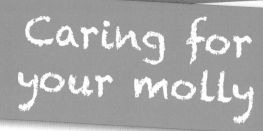

Caring for your molly

Most mollies survive best in water that has some salt in it. The salt can help keep your fish healthy by killing many of the diseases that mollies get.

Mollies do best in a large fish tank in which they can easily swim around without becoming bored.

Keep lots of rocks in your fish tank. Mollies love to explore and will often hide inside little caves and any cracks and holes between rocks.

Some mollies are white with black spots.

28

Step 4

Now add even more detail to the fish's body. Keep a steady hand as you draw the tiny scales and add fine lines to the fins. Then give your molly a dark, beady eye.

Step 5

Complete your picture with color. Use shades of yellow, then add some black, dark green, and blue. Lighter areas will give your drawing some depth. Don't forget to give the eye a dark-colored rim.

Glossary

aggressive: likely to attack

ancient: from a long time ago

aquarium salt: a type of salt that is suitable for fish tanks

beady: like a bead

bred: mated with another to produce babies

coral: a rocklike structure made of animal skeletons

detail: the fine pencil markings on a drawing

environment: an area in which something lives

explore: to discover more about a place

fake: not real

filter: a device that removes waste from water

fin: part of a fish that helps it to swim through water

freshwater: water that does not contain salt, such as river water

gill: the part of a fish that helps it to take oxygen from water

markings: the patterns on an animal's fur, feathers, or scales

nostril: the opening through which something breathes

oxygen: a gas that most creatures need to breathe to survive

palette: a range of colors

poisoned: made very ill by contact with a dangerous substance

predator: creature that hunts other creatures for food

proportion: the size of one part of the body in relation to another

salt water: water that contains salt, such as seawater

sea anemone: sea-living animal with poisonous tentacles

shading: pencil strokes that add depth to a picture

shoal: group of the same species of fish

species: a type of animal or plant

tentacle: armlike structure on a sea-living animal

For More Information

Books

Blackaby, Susan. *Fish for You: Caring for Your Fish*. Minneapolis, MN: Picture Window Books, 2003.

Grob, John-Marc. *How to Draw and Color Fish*. JMG Studio, 2011.

Lee, Justin. *How to Draw Fish*. New York, NY: PowerKids Press, 2002.

Schuetz, Kari. *Caring for Your Fish*. Minneapolis, MN: Bellwether Media, 2010.

Websites

Find out more about keeping goldfish at:
www.fishkeeping.co.uk/articles_35/goldfish.htm

Discover more about how to keep tropical fish at:
carolord.hubpages.com/hub/Tropical-fish-keeping-for-beginnerschildren-create-your-own-underwater-world

Learn more about fish at:
www.kidskonnect.com/subject-index/13-animals/30-fish.html

Index